MYSTERIES

OF THE

UNIVERSE

by Lela Nargi

raintree

a Capstone company — publishers for children

Raintree is an imprint of Capstone Global Library Limited, a company incorporated in England and Wales having its registered office at 264 Banbury Road, Oxford, OX2 7DY – Registered company number: 6695582

www.raintree.co.uk
myorders@raintree.co.uk

Edited by Hank Musolf
Designed by Sara Radka
Original illustrations © Capstone Global Library Limited 2021
Picture research by Jo Miller
Production by Laura Manthe
Originated by Capstone Global Library Ltd
Printed and bound in India

978 1 3982 0479 9 (hardback)
978 1 3982 0478 2 (paperback)

British Library Cataloguing in Publication Data
A full catalogue record for this book is available from the British Library.

Acknowledgements
We would like to thank the following for permission to reproduce photographs: Anand Raichoor (Federal Polytechnic of Lausanne, Switzerland) and the SDSS collaboration, 21, (Top); ESO: Digitized Sky Survey 2 Acknowledgement: Davide De Martin, 21, (Bottom); Newscom: Album/20TH CENTURY FOX, 27; Science Source: Atlas Photo Bank, 9, Emilio Segrè Visual Archives / American Institute of Physics, 15, Mark Garlick, 13, 22-23, Royal Institution of Great Britain, 8; Shutterstock: Denis Belitsky, 20, Designua, 11, Diego Cervo, 29, Everett Historical, 6, GiroScience, 26, IM_photo, 5, MaraZe, 15 (Inset), Vadim Sadovski, Cover, Vikulin, 5 (Inset); Wikimedia: ESO/M. Kornmesser, 25, F Schmutzer, 7, NASA, 16, (Top Inset), 16, 19 (Inset), NASA and the European Space Agency., 19, R. Williams (STScI), the HDF-S Team, and NASA/ESA, 16, (Bottom Inset). Design elements: Shutterstock: Anna Kutukova, Aygun Ali

CONTENTS

Words in **bold** are in the glossary.

CHAPTER 1

THE START OF EVERYTHING

Imagine some squirrels sitting in a tree. Think about a friend practising tuba in space, and then a faraway galaxy. What do these things have in common? They are all part of the universe. So is the **gravity** holding the squirrels on their tree. So are the deep parts of space where you can't hear tuba sounds. So is the galaxy so far away that it's hard to imagine. The universe is made up of everything.

But where did the seed that made the tree come from? Or the squirrels? Or the elements that give us light and energy? Can we trace the universe to where it began? Scientists have learned a lot about the universe over thousands of years. But there are still mysteries they are trying to solve.

Aristotle

BACK TO THE BEGINNING

Did the universe actually begin? Or has it always been around? This has been a very hot topic for a very long time. Many ancient people thought their gods made the universe.

Aristotle was sure the universe had always existed. He was a Greek philosopher in the 300s BC. He did not think you could get everything out of nothing. Fast forward 2,000 years to England. In the 1600s, scientist Isaac Newton agreed with Aristotle. So did scientist Albert Einstein 218 years later. Both physicists also believed that the universe was always the same size. It was **static**.

Albert Einstein

CHAPTER 2

SO MANY QUESTIONS

Isaac Newton discovered gravity in 1687 by studying objects falling. Soon after, he had another big question. Is the universe **finite** or **infinite**? Does it have edges like a table? Or does it stretch forever? Where does it go?

Isaac Newton

Newton knew gravity pulls everything towards everything else. But gravity would make a finite and static universe collapse. That wasn't happening, though.

Einstein also wondered about this question. His calculations showed the universe expanding. But that couldn't happen if it were static. What was going on?

Galaxies move apart as the universe expands.

TWO UNIVERSAL DISCOVERIES

Our view of the universe became clearer in the 1920s. That's when scientists made two huge discoveries.

Light from faraway space objects has really long **wavelengths**. This means those objects are moving. So much for a static universe! Those wavelengths get longer when an object is further away. This means the universe is expanding. Everything in it moves away from everything else. Astronomers measure these wavelengths by using telescopes at different times. When Earth is in a different position, the telescopes can get different views. They see that the wavelengths get longer, showing when the object moves further away.

Balloons can help show
how the universe expands.

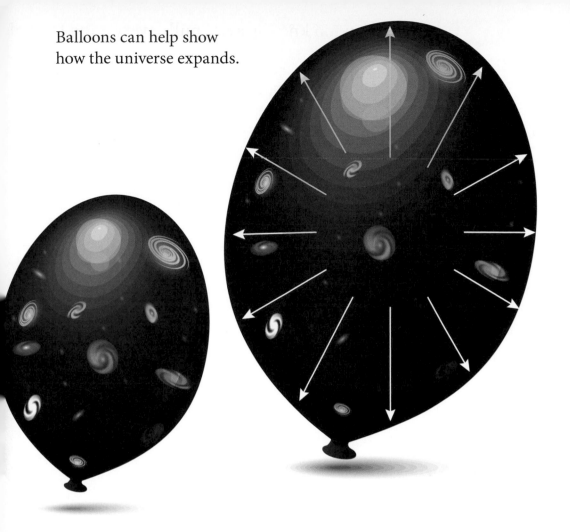

A universe that's moving means two interesting
things. First, the universe was once much smaller.
Second, something must have made it start moving.

CHAPTER 3

THE UNIVERSE IS BORN

About 13.8 billion years ago, most scientists believe there was nothing. Shortly after, 13.7 billion years ago, the Big Bang happened. It instantly set the brand new universe in motion like fireworks going off.

Before scientists knew there even was a Big Bang, they had many theories. They weren't sure how the universe began, but they agreed that there was nothing before the universe started.

Many scientists had found clues to the Big Bang in their work. But they hadn't believed the clues. Einstein called this his "greatest blunder".

MYSTERY FACT

The early universe could not grow until it cooled to 5,432 degrees Celsius (3,000 degrees Fahrenheit).

300,000 yrs

300 million yrs

9 billion yrs

13.7 billion yrs

The universe's evolution from the Big Bang (left) to the present day (right)

CHAPTER 4

HUBBLE'S LAW

Scientists continued studying the universe in the 1900s. But astronomer Edwin Hubble saw something else through his telescope. He saw that faraway stars were moving at different speeds. He discovered that galaxies that are further from us move faster than galaxies that are closer to us. This is called Hubble's Law. The universe does not expand into space that exists. Space expands, though. Every day in our universe, more something is made from nothing.

Pretend you are making a cake. The cake is the universe. You mix raisins into the mixture. The raisins are galaxies. The cake puffs up as it bakes. This makes the raisins move away from one another. That is like the universe expanding.

Edwin Hubble

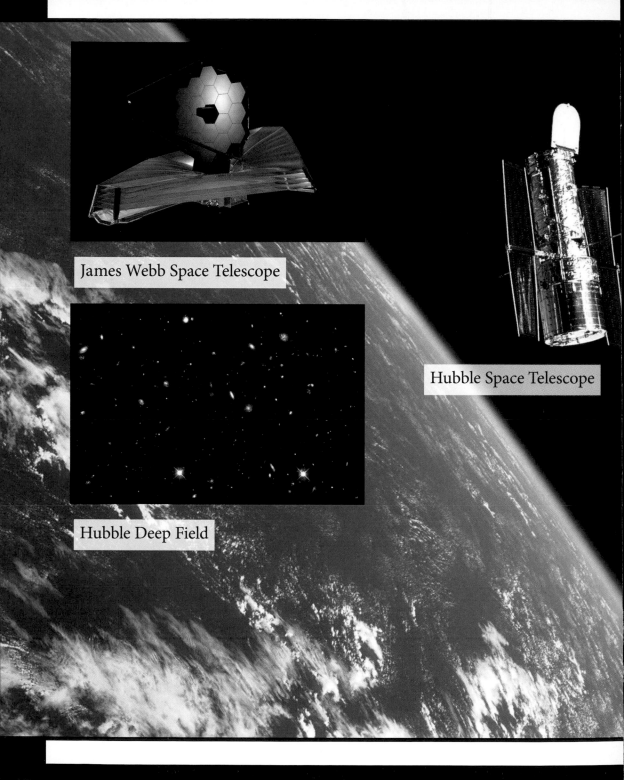

James Webb Space Telescope

Hubble Space Telescope

Hubble Deep Field

HUBBLE'S TELESCOPE

Edwin Hubble died in 1953. But his name lives on in the Hubble Space Telescope.

NASA launched it in 1990. It takes pictures from its **orbit** 611.5 km (380 miles) above Earth. One area the Hubble can see is called the Hubble Deep Field. It is 13 billion light years away! Those pictures helped scientists learn the age of the universe. Now they are helping us to see its size. They are helping us to see how it has changed over time. Hubble's job is to answer some of the biggest mysteries of the universe. The James Webb Space Telescope will join it in 2021.

MYSTERY FACT

Hubble's most famous photograph is of thousands of galaxies set against a dark piece of distant sky.

CHAPTER 5

THE EMPTY SPACE

The universe has stars, moons, planets, meteors, black holes and galaxies. Meteors are rocks that fly through space. Black holes are places in space with strong gravity that pull in anything close. Galaxies are collections of stars, planets and many more space objects.

If you picture the universe as vegetable soup in a big bowl, what else makes up the soup of the universe? What is in that "empty" space between the planets and stars?

The answer is gas. Ninety-two per cent of the gas in the universe is hydrogen. The rest is mostly helium. Hydrogen and helium have been with us since the universe was three minutes old.

The Hubble Telescope can see up
to 15 billion light years away.

HOW BIG IS THE UNIVERSE?

How big is the universe? We do not really know. But scientists do have some **hypotheses** (guesses based on science).

The visible universe is what we can see from Earth with all our tools. Scientists think it is 93 billion light years across. But it could be bigger. It could be infinite.

The universe is billions of times bigger than when it was just starting. And we know it is getting bigger all the time.

LIGHT YEARS

A light year measures how far light can travel in one year. That is 9 trillion km (5.6 trillion miles). It would take a spaceship 4.2 light years to get to Alpha Centauri. That is the next closest star after our Sun. It would take 200,000 light years to cross our Milky Way galaxy.

WHAT'S IN A SHAPE?

Scientists do not know what shape the universe is. They cannot even see most of it. They have some hypotheses about its shape. These have to do with **density**. Density is how big an object is compared to how much matter it has. A heavy bowling ball has more density than a football filled with air.

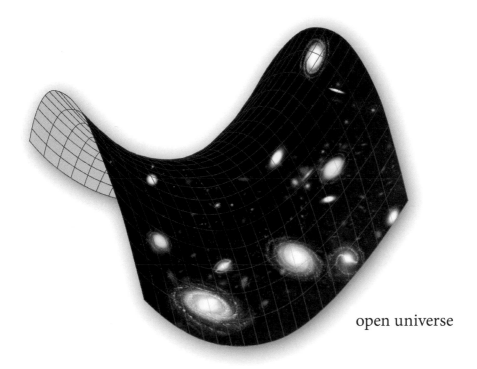

open universe

An open universe has low density. It can expand forever. It has a curved shape like a saddle for a horse.

closed universe

A closed universe has high density. It will one day stop expanding. It is shaped like a globe.

flat universe

A flat universe has medium density. It will stop expanding very slowly. It is thin like a pancake. Scientists believe we are in a flat universe.

FASTER THAN A SPEEDING UNIVERSE

How fast is the universe expanding? Some scientists worked that out in 2017.

They made a measurement that showed that objects 3.3 million light years apart move 73 km (46 miles) per second. It was based on how bright **quasars** are. They are the brightest things in the universe. Other scientists are not sure about this measurement. They agree the universe is moving faster than we thought.

One day we will look through telescopes and the only stars we will see will be in our own galaxy. All the others will be too far away.

A single quasar can have thousands of times more energy than our galaxy.

QUASARS

Quasars live in the centre of galaxies. They get their energy from supermassive black holes. Scientists have found 190,000 of them so far.

CHAPTER 6

A LONELY COSMOS

Are we living in the only universe? What would other universes look like? One theory is that others could be duplicate universes. In them we would find a duplicate of everything in our universe, including ourselves. Some scientists theorize it could be possible.

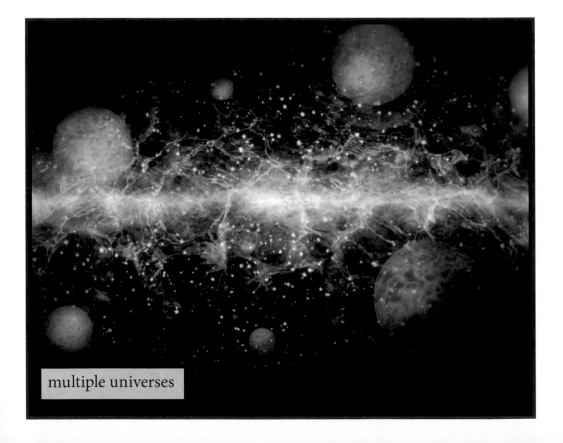

multiple universes

What if the Big Bang made a multiverse, or multiple universes? There are also theories on the different types of multiverses we could have. One is infinite universes. They all look the same. They go on forever.

Parallel universes are another theory. They lie side by side. Scientists continue to study all sorts of mysterious theories about the nature of our universe, and theories about universes we don't know about yet help us understand ours better. For example, the study of theories of multiple universes helps us understand what happened during the Big Bang better.

MYSTERY FACT

Cosmos is another word for the universe.

In *The Chronicles of Narnia*, characters travelled to a parallel universe.

CHAPTER 7

RIP, FREEZE, CRUNCH AND BOUNCE

Do you get the feeling that the more we learn about the universe, the less we know? Scientists still have so many questions.

They want to know how fast the universe really is expanding. They want to study if there were multiple Big Bangs. What will happen to the universe in trillions of years? Will it break apart with a big rip? Will it expand so far that it stops moving in a big freeze? Will it start shrinking and end in a big crunch?

We might never know the answers to all of these questions. But that won't stop scientists from trying to work it out.

What questions do you still have about the universe? Maybe one day you can help find the answers!

GLOSSARY

density amount of mass an object or substance has based on a unit of volume

finite has an end

gravity force that pulls objects with mass together; gravity pulls objects down towards the centre of Earth

hypothesis prediction that can be tested about how a scientific investigation or experiment will turn out

infinite something that goes on forever

light year how long it takes light to travel in a year

orbit path an object follows as it goes around the Sun or a planet

quasar mass in space that gives off light; quasars are larger than stars but smaller than galaxies

static always the same

wavelength distances between two peaks of a wave

FIND OUT MORE

BOOKS

Aliens, UFOs and Other Mysteries from Space (Mystery Solvers), Sarah Levete (Raintree, 2020)

The Mysteries of the Universe: Discover the best-kept secrets of space, DK (DK Children, 2020)

Solar System (DKfindout!), Sarah Cruddas (DK Children, 2016)

WEBSITES

www.bbc.co.uk/bitesize/topics/zdrrd2p
Discover more about the solar system.

www.dkfindout.com/uk/space/stars-and-galaxies
Find out more about stars and galaxies.

www.esa.int/kids/en/home
Learn more about space from the European Space Agency.

INDEX